Inner Outer

A Poetry Collection

By
B. Brunswick

ISBN: 978-0-6480808-7-9

To Maggie and Jaclyn
for help, inspiration and friendship.

Warning
This book contains bad language

Introduction

What is the nature of humanity? To explore; to explore the world around us, the cosmos and what lives inside us.

Only through exploration can we find freedom, happiness and live out our dreams.

We are going on a journey together where even the sky is not the limit. It is real, it is true, it is you and it is me. Let's explore the good, the bad, the world and humanity. Lets journey through dreams, space and time. Let's discover what makes us, us.

Come with me through the inner and the outer, it will be a wild ride!

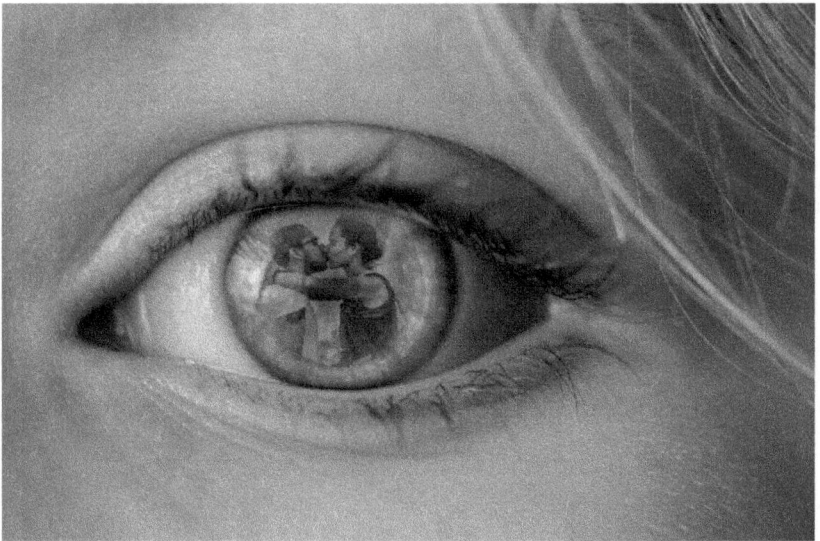

Inner Outer

When you're searching for something

To fill up your nothing

To open up your eyes that are closed.

You can't believe what you're seeing, when it's living and
breathing

And standing in front of your nose.

Hidden mind behind a front door

If you're too scared to explore

The possibilities that are endless and grand.

You'd rather just know it, than possibly blow it

And it's slipping like time through your hands.

Will you break through this prison?

Will you be forgiven?

Will you be happy to be misunderstood?

Will anyone listen, or clear up your vision

And know you're on a journey for good?

You think it's all outer

When most of it's inner

Do you hold on to a glimmer of hope?

You're consciousness drifting, liberating, uplifting

And you'll be glad from the day you awoke.

Now there's no more illusion

But far more confusion

Can you be wrong and not even care?

The mind can be deceiving, because you don't believe it

Doesn't mean that the truth isn't there.

When All the Love Dies

What will become of the world when all the love dies?

What will become of us if we only live to hate?

Will we be stranded under ever-darkening skies?

Will we destroy more than we create?

Will the bitterness of tears keep rolling from our eyes?

Will we cease to give and only proceed to take?

Will we breathe these neverending lies?

Will we fight for those we love, and those that we fight, are those we hate?

Will sorrow burn and consume us all,

When we wallow in the grief of death?

Will the hate of humans make us fall?

Will the mistakes we make leave love bereft?

Will we all suffer the fate of fools, or will those fools consume the rest?

Will thunder rattle our stony walls, to leave us all so short of breath?

Will the fangs of evil consume our souls?

The shadows and blackness, swallow the light?

Will the earth open up, and swallow us whole?

Will the darkness grow and then, take flight?

Will the whistling wind be howling and cold?

Will the daytime become an endless night?

Will we feed greedily off the fear we hold?

Will we stand strong, learn all our lessons,

Or will we crumble, will we fold?

Will every lost person cry for no reason?

Will every dreamer stand up and thrive?

Will every lost soul float through the seasons?

How many lost souls are barely alive?

Stealing the moments, the ones left to cling to

Stealing a breath, taking our time

Walking at midnight, talking at twilight

Struggling over the cold divide

Standing together, the light burns forever,

Only then can love survive.

Oxygen Thief

You could spread the love, but you don't
You could lift them up, you won't
You could give them more, more than you know
You could help them along the hard, rocky road

You could spread the light, but you're scared
The toughest of shells, is never to care
You could give so much, if you only dared
You could be good, but inside your dead

Do you hate when you're alone in the night?
Do you spit your lies, spill out all your spite?
Do you kick, and scream, and endlessly fight?
Do you bellow when you know you're not right?

Fear, does it rule you, controlling your mind?
Are you a fool, an idiot, ignorant or are you just blind?
Why do you see what you do, through those eyes?
To keep pushing the hate, and keep spreading the lies?

Do you fear fellow creatures, are you a freak?
Do you believe the words, the bullshit you speak?
Are you a dark soul, are you a creep?
Are you standing up tall but down in a heap?

Do you lie to yourself every day?
Are you loving yourself all the way?
Do use broken souls for your play?
Are you using the weak for your prey?

Are you passing the knowledge you hold?
Are you living, or just growing old?
Are you a lost, forgotten, long lonely soul?
Are you the darkness, inside you're cold?

What you're putting out there, you become
If you live by the sword, you'll die by the gun
The brave will stand up tall, the cowards will run
You love to watch them crumble then you'll be done.

You could spread the love, but you don't

You could lift them up, you won't

You could give them more, more than you know

You could help them along the hard, rocky road

You could spread the light, but your scared

The toughest of shells is never to care

You could give so much, if you only dared

You could be good, but inside your dead

Rose and the Soldier

"Come over here my Rose, oh my darling

Come over here to the place that I lay

I'm overcome with the coldest of shadows

Come hold my hand, as my spirit does fade

Come over here and kneel by my bedside

This will be the last time you gaze upon my face

Oh, come over here to fill me with comfort

My heart it is broken and I'm dying today."

"I care no more for the fate of my body

I fear not the reaper, have no concept of hell

Sit by my side 'til the crack in the morning

Soak up my words, my story to tell

Don't close your eyes, don't miss one more moment

Don't weep for me, in the battle I fell

My body is broken, my blood is escaping

My spirit is fading, this body a shell."

"Carry each word for your life ever longer

Carry each smile, each glint in the eye

Our love will live on, wherever you wander

Our love will live on, please Rose don't cry

I see the black smoke invade the horizon

My breath it grows short, my mouth it goes dry

See me not for this body that's broken

Just finish this dream 'fore the long endless night."

Why? (The Soldiers Burial)

We shed a tear for our fallen sons

Where the bullets fly

The days draw in, the winter comes

And we don't know why

Blood it stains the soil

We close our eyes

The blood flows like a river

And we don't know why. There is no reason why.

The hatred calls

From within us all

Cold tears we cry

The sorrow burns, the left will learn

That they don't know why

And now it seems in haunted dreams

We're running out of time

And now the shadows spread inside our heads

And invade our minds

And we don't know why. There is no reason why.

As long as men will walk the earth

We'll live and fight and die

The ones we love left standing there

And they don't know why.

How can we face the truth?

We close our eyes

How can we accept the fact,

We don't know why? There is no reason why.

The Statue Boy

He was born and became a statue.

He sat high on the hill with his other statue friends.

He watched the world changing endless below him.

He watched the summers change to winters,

And then turn back again.

One by one his statue friends, broke their bonds and all at once they were free.

No longer stuck, trapped upon the hilltop.

Skipped gayly through the forests, then the mountains, and away towards the sea.

A stony tear fell from his lonely eye, as the rain and wind ripped at his face.

It whipped against his barricade.

The weight of rock imprisoned him still and more,

As the hope he held, could do little else but fade.

He was lonesome and cold, he was forgotten and subdued.

Without reason his hatred started to consume him.

His form so hard, his body cold and nude.

His statue friends returned to mock him.

They pointed fingers, hurled their insults.

He said not a word, he cried bitterly inside.

His skin showed the cracks of time,

His heart showed the wounds of fault.

A hundred winters entrapped him, until he no longer saw the sun.

His hatred ate away at him

No laughs, no joy, no hope to escape, no hope for him to run.

On the coldest night of the coldest year, when the wind howled at the moon.

A good soul came to heal him, she was beauty and she loved him.

She wished his dreams mapped out before him

She wished to free him from his tomb.

His stone heart fluttered as she smiled and gazed into his frozen
eyes.

And like she had bewitched him

From his stone heart, a fire grew inside.

Slowly day by day his prison started to crumble

As the stars burned, finally, he woke from his stony sleep.

And tumbled down the hilltop.

At long last because she loved him, the statue boy was free.

Broken Heart

The skin from my days that drips cold from my bones

A million friends evade, I end up alone

These seconds mean nothing

As these seconds depart

All that is left, is me and my broken heart.

The silence surrounds me as my hopes disappear

Flowing out of mouth and into deaf ears

The mountains collide, I look to the stars

There is nothing left, but me and my broken heart.

If the future seems empty with no words left to say

No sign of tomorrow, little hope for today

My body is fallen, attacked by the plague

Bounded and broken, left tears in my wake

All that is left is this cold map of scars

My words and my soul and my broken heart

A volcano's exploding, I wish to explain

The things that I want, the words I can't say

Life's cauldron just bubbles, as cold as the rain

A cloud of confusion to cover my pain

The tears will run free, if they ever start

All I have now is me and my broken heart

If I could wish for more from the time

But time is a prison that's trapping my mind

The rivers that flow more mountains collide

Forgotten and frozen, a slave to my pride

And the memories end before they can start

And all that's left over is me and my broken heart

Prison is heaven when you're on your death bed

When doubt is forgotten and there ain't nothing left

With surging on endless 'til the day of your death

The pain in the heart, the shortness of breath

My future left shattered by fate's poisoned dart

And all that is left is me and my broken heart.

Blowing Kisses

Will the light come flooding in?

Will the hopeful stop the rain?

Will the beast that taunts my soul,

Ever show its face again?

Will this journey last forever?

Will the sorrow ever fade?

I'm waving goodbye to the tears,

And blowing kisses to my pain.

Will this distant dream come true?

Will this feeling keep me sane?

Will this forgotten, broken promise,

Go dripping down the drain?

Does the sunlight warm my soul?

In the moonlight will I sway?

Am I floating on the ocean?

Am I cold or am I grey?

I'm waving goodbye to my tears,

And blowing kisses to my pain.

Will the silence ever find me?

Will my last nerve end up frayed?

Will I walk out to tomorrow,

And forget about today?

Will the wounds that mark my body,

These scars that mark my brain,

Take me rolling on forever,

Or drag me down again?

I'm waving goodbye to my tears,

And blowing kisses to my pain.

Do You Love?

Are you a special person, do you do amazing things?

Do you pass on all your wisdom, or spread the joy you bring?

Do you look at your reflection, and like the face you see?

Are you endlessly improving, are you happy, are you free?

Are the shadows in the distance, or are you fumbling in the dark?

Do you empower other people, or are you always breaking
hearts?

The journey never ending, the richness turns to wealth

But before you go any further, do you love yourself?

You're giving, you're forgiving, you're generous and kind

The smiles upon your face but the doubt is in your mind

Have you stewed on, stuck in silence, have the jokers caught your
gaze?

Have you spent your time just waiting, and ticking off the days?

The oceans full of wonder, you won't see 'til you dive in

The bravest face you can muster, and a hurricane within

The sparkles lose their lustre when the truth is somewhere else

Before the journey can continue, do you love yourself?

You're amazing, you're a wonder, you're a brightly shining star

Remember no surrender and be proud of what you are

Sing it from the roof tops, own all the things you do

Reach out to forever and become the proper you

See with childlike wonder, with those sparkles in your eyes

Being human's never easy, and neither is this life

Time to spread some goodness before we end up on the shelf

Life's a game you can win if you only love yourself.

Fuckin Asshole!

The times when you feel like you've made it

It titillates a soul that is dead

You sit and you dream of a better life

When you'll go from this, to a mess

You sit and you pout, raise the atmosphere

You don't worry about the hearts of the rest

When you fuck up man, it's spectacular!

And it's not long 'til your fuckin up next

So you're high on mist and on collusion

And you think it makes you naughty and bad

But the thing that you love is an illusion

And despite what you think, you're still sad

You can spit out the very best friendships

It's easier to get attention from men

And you know it won't be so long 'til

You'll be a fuckin asshole again.

You're laughing outside, at sweet nothing

You've fallen like a long-lingered dream

But the shadows are gathering near you

And you don't even know what they mean

You think you're true to yourself and true to the others

When you lie to yourself every day

The truth will always put out the fire

But you know no other way

Extracting what you want from the cosmos

And fuckin off what comes to pass

While the clown that looks back from the mirror

Will be kicking your cold lonely ass

And you spit out your soul all too easy

With a shimmering shield of pretend

You'll welcome the low and the sleazy

And be a fuckin asshole again.

You're not proud of the things you are doing

But your vision is so bent and so blurred

You mistake loving for screwing

And you're mistaking actions with words

Now cry one more time, you have done it

Now everyone's world is ripped apart

And now it's time to put on the stitching

And sew up you're broken old heart

Take that sorrow, that silence, that empty

And turn daggers for eyes but unfelt

You're hating everybody so gently

But the only person you hate, is yourself

You can cry and have hugs, and have sorrow

You can pretend once again you have friends

But we all know come another tomorrow

You'll be a fuckin asshole again.

The fires getting snubbed out, forever

The fire isn't real, but it burns in your head

It's spreading, it's growing forever

It'll burn you 'til there ain't nothing left

The inferno of life will consume you

In fact, it already has

The clouds that are rolling around you

Are the only comfort you have

You can try and escape from your sorrow

You can spend some time learning what's true

Everyone knows that you're running

But you'll never run faster than you

The walls all around you a prison

The walls that can only contain

And purity may be your vision

But you're a fuckin asshole again.

Now you stare at the wall in your sadness

And you wonder how it all went so wrong

It was a car crash, just waiting to happen

And you have just lingered too long

You cry and the tears they taste bitter

You use deception to brighten your life

But when it all falls apart, you are broken

Cos your judgement, it cuts like a knife

It crumbles down like it had to

It shatters your glass-like thick skin

And you're the one destroying your own life

Maybe try doing some good honest things

And you think you've been treated unkindly

You have by yourself, my lost friend

And you did it to brighten your existence

But you were a fuckin asshole again.

Who?

Who are you?

Now is the time to find out

How are you?

Behind a wall of doubt

Where are you,

In the head or in the heart?

What are you,

If you don't know where to start?

Who are you?

Are you standing in your way?

How are you?

Fallen, lead astray

Where are you?

Somewhere in the mist

What are you?

A soul that's set adrift.

Who are you?

Are you cold and lost on the path?

How are you?

The joker always laughs

Where are you?

The head up in the clouds

What are you?

Scream it loud and proud

Who are you?

Now the mountains looming large

How are you?

Reaching for the stars

Where are you?

Just looking for the way

What are you?

When there's nothing left to say

Who are you?

Are you hollow, are you full?

How are you?

Are you silent or a fool?

Where are you?

Float the cosmos in the mind

What are you?

It's what we're tryna find

Who are you?

Searching all the time

How are you?

Are you open, are you blind?

Where are you?

Somewhere we don't know

What are you?

Swimming against the flow

Who are you?

Time to find the truth

How are you?

Looking for the proof

Where are you?

Free from all the doubt

What are you?

It's the time for finding out

What is True?

Will you explore the cosmos?

Will you explore your mind?

Will you break down all the barriers?

And not fear what it is you find?

Will you break this illusion?

Will you cry out for hope?

Will you be lost inside confusion,

And be blinded by the smoke?

Will the walls turn into freedom?

Will the shackles set you free?

Will you accept a life of wisdom?

And shoot it on the breeze?

Will you be coming back soon,

Or have you lost your mind?

Will the shadows endless consume,

Or will you step towards the light?

Will the future open up its arms,

And accept just what you are?

Brave, true and determined

And heading for the stars.

Do you look out to the nothing?

Is there nothing there to see?

Are you proud and hold your head high,

At the dreams in which you weave?

Are you waiting there for no one?

Are you open like the sea?

Are you willing to be wrong,

And forget what you believe?

How Many Summers do you Have Left?

How many dreams have been left to shadows?

How many swallowed, shallow breaths?

How many lost souls do we fight for tomorrow?

Their love, their light, their hope bereft.

How many times did you touch the sunrise?

How many summers do you have left?

How many dreams fall by the wayside?

How many shadows are twisted, cracked and vexed?

How many winters do you sit and shiver?

How many gone, how many next?

How many dreams are here left to cling to?

How many mornings 'til you face your death?

Can you catch those dreams or are you gonna waste them?

How many summers do have left?

Fallen and broken, looking for no one

Silent, so frozen, unfucked and unslept.

How many futures given up for wisdom?

How many wasted however many steps?

Surge forever, surge 'til the morning.

By low light, by midnight they wept.

How many times do you have left to fail?

How many summers do you have left?

Humankind

There isn't much kind about humans

There's so little good about man

As we tease and we rape mother earth

Slashing and burning the land.

We spout hate through judgement in believing

While we bask in that we achieve

But we achieve nothing at all that is useful

We just poison the air that we breath.

We hate our neighbours because of their colour

We hate all our friends with our envy

We kill each other for ideology

We die for that which we dream.

We're all killers and thieves and liars

When we all just care for ourselves

I'd open them all up expose all their souls

If I ever even dreamed it would help.

Over breeding always feeding the population

So our human disease ever spreads

Some possess all you could wish for

Others not even been fed.

We stand and we bask in our own glory

We think we're amazing and noble and grand

Yet still we end up in the dirt

As the future slips right through our hands.

Do gooding and then we look downwards

The statement they make is so great

But what are you taking their lives for,

When they're just other creatures of hate?

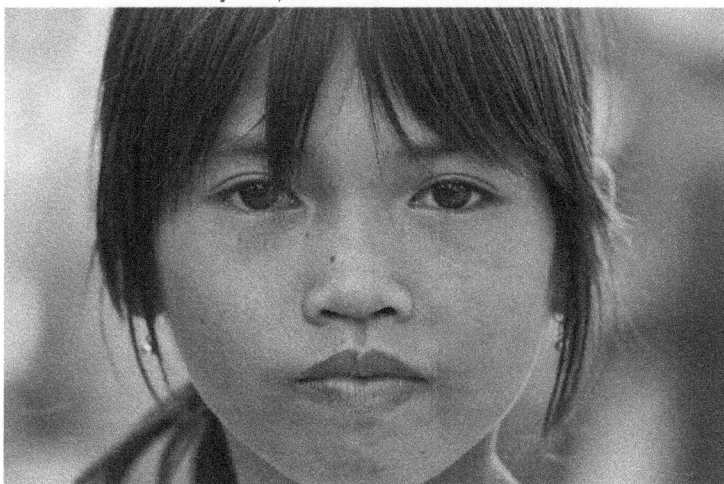

Conscious Drifting

Where do I live?

In my heart, in my head?

Imagining everything,

And traveling the cosmos in my bed.

Is this sea of endless nothing,

An ocean full of shining stars,

A void or coloured chasm,

Or a billion beating hearts?

Where do I live?

In my body, in my mind?

Or is this meat that surrounds me,

All there is to find?

I crossed barriers and bridges

And split through the divide.

I walk a million miles

But I never leave inside.

Where do we live?

On Earth, in time, in space?

Drifting like a memory.

Swiftly from place to place.

Will this place remain our prison?

Is this place all there is?

Before we ever find out.

We all have a life to live.

Changing the World

Psycho snapping, spamming reality
Freaks are scanning the night
Pricks and fools, that seem so melodic
The fuelled and the full, and the bang to rights

Seeming so lost when you've had a victory
One of these days some shit's gotta change
Forgotten and fallen and reaching for destiny
The path it has crumbled, a life rearranged

Thick like a milkshake, dense as the atmosphere
Losing all sight of the fools and the cruel
You might end up flying right into the stratosphere
You might end up losing but you'll give it your all

Time to change for one and for others
Time to break free in the shackles we're held
If they climb up high to the top of the mountain
Hand in hand could change the world

Crossroads

Crossroads on journeys

Junctions in time

Forgotten horizons

As we float through the night

We lie looking backwards

Mind flipping the days

Ghosts from the past

Dead rise from your graves

Every word uttered carves us

The statue that is grown

Each second we're together

More vital than we know

These crossroads are endless

Etched lines on the map

The map on our faces

The weights on our backs

The smiles that light us

The tears that tare our souls

The times we climbed the mountain.

When we're huddled in a hole

Each and every chance encounter

Creates a moment just the same

Even if you forget their face

Or you never knew their name

Everyone who tried to cut you

They made you brave and made you strong

The ones that always shunned you

Made you know where you belong

Even the dark and cruel that broke you

Or those who broke your heart

They made you who you are now

They all play an equal part

These crossroads that we come to

Each second of our lives

They can put you in the gutter

Or make you glad that you're alive.

Shit Storm

Through the lies that are threaded round the hopes of the
abandoned
Have a use for the frailties of the broken, your own
Twisting the knife and twisting more 'til pain is normal
The illusion of wholeness and pipe dreams of home.

The vultures are circling if you welcome them always
Destroying yourself in a bid to be free
The shadows of doubt the cold lonely truth
You're too scared to reason, too scared to see.

A hurricane's been round here and I'm not sure what happened
The shit storm of hate circles my door
You came inside this world's blown apart
You took all you could, and then came back for more.

Moulded

Reaching out for the silent horizon

The fate that can fuck with your mind

Avoiding the hate, the grief and the violence

Making the most of the time

The right to hear, if the truth remains silent

The old, the weary and wise

The childish ones are the cold lonely island

Alone and barely alive

Taking these steps that may lead to nowhere

The pathway that is never set

Taking a leap that may lead to somewhere

And it's banging inside of your head

Fallen divides that mess with your selfcare

Your legs are as heavy as lead

The heart that is broken, needing some repair

But there isn't any glue left

The map on your face, the scars in your being

Show the story of where you have been

And even if you don't know what you are seeing

You're living this life like a dream

The shadow is here, the people are fleeing

And they don't even know what it means

As gravity crushes the cold and the seething

You can gently paddle downstream

With eye's full of love our souls ever hoping

The dream we could ever be free

With the blackening skies on pollution we're choking

And we're setting adrift on the sea

This life it comes and ends before we're woken

It adds up to one memory

And the souls of the fallen, the bad and the broken

Become what they wanted to be

Humankind II

Draw your strength from me my brother
My sister, my neighbour, my friend
We're crying through these tragic times
We're the shit that lives in men.

The ashes ever settle
On this never-ending war
Our hearts are always breaking
And we're rotten to the core

The tears we shed in hunger
From wanting ever more
The light of which we cling to
Is cold and so unsure

Take my hand my brothers
Why do you hate us all so much?
We all breathe the same polluted air
We eat, we drink, we fuck

Your gods have all flown away
They have forsaken us
All your gods are judging you
While your gods are judging us

Take my hands my brothers
Let's all live for all we're worth
Let's walk side by side now
We're all children of this earth.

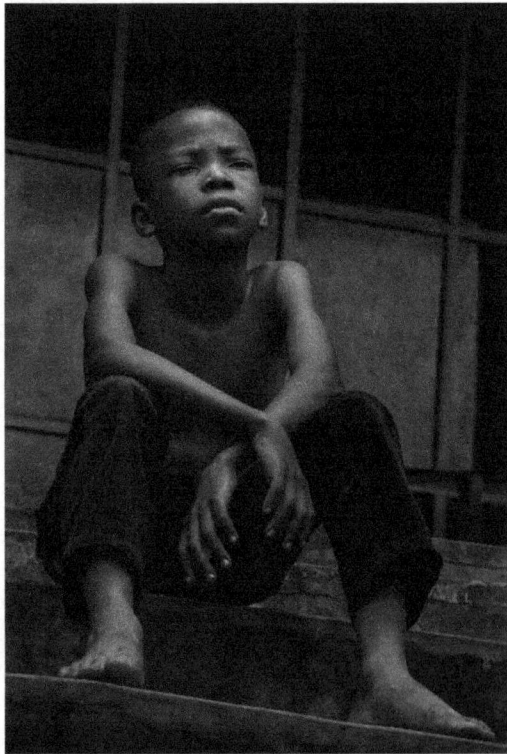

A Million Miles Away

Time it ticks ever slowly

Wild oceans keep us apart

There's always something missing

In an ever-heavy heart

Telling tales of the yester years, spinning yarns about the past

How I wish that I was with you

How I wish that I could fly

As I march towards the sunset

In this ever-blackened sky

Your voices, taunting my tomorrow

Tears are welling in my eyes

My dreams stretched out before me

My dreams that disappear

My stony soul that crumbles

My heavy heart is trapped right here

The future seems forever

Through the weeks and through the years

My loneliness that haunts me

My hollow happiness upon my face

The sun is burning brightly

But my shadows in my wake

The doubt etched upon the horizon

As I drift through time and space

Onwards I must journey

I strive just to ignore

My eyes locked upon the raging ocean

From this misty shore

Every time I see you

I always long for more

In the end the time will catch me

In the moonlight I will sway

As I'm staring through tomorrow

I'm trapped inside today

My world it seems so empty

From a million miles away

Connections

Golden lines that surly bind us

Golden memories to make

Waffle doesn't blind us

If it's real or really fake

Golden lines that connect us

A golden bond of trust

The warmth will not forget us

When we're bathing in the love

Golden lines that always reach us

Golden stars that twinkle bright

Wisdom there to teach us

On a long and lonely night

Golden lines that stretch towards us

And wrap around our soul

The smiles that reward us

And never lose their hold

Golden friendships always take us

Connecting two bright shining stars

The value won't escape us

Gold connections to our hearts

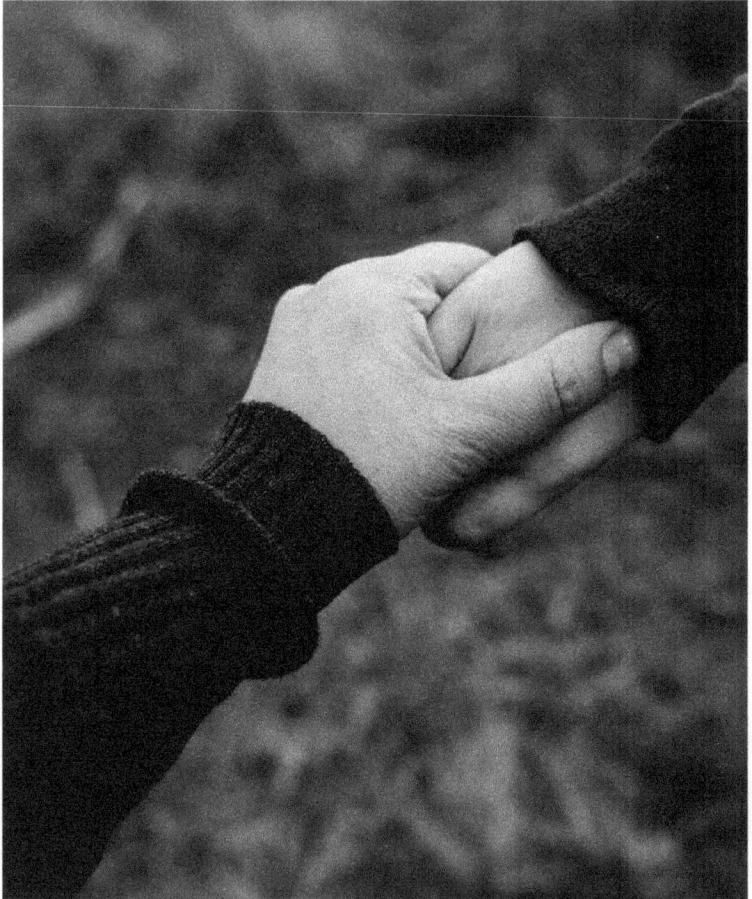

Sleepless Dreams

"Won't you stay a little longer?"

"I can't cos it's not real."

"Will you come back here forever?"

"I won't, I'm standing still."

"Won't you change the world for better?"

"I can't, I have no voice."

"Will another night bring us together?"

"Every time, if it was my choice."

"Does the pain burn in your heart now?"

"It's burning ever more."

"Won't you see the shooting star?"

"I'll watch from the misty shore."

"Which pathway have you chosen?"

"The one I know the least."

"Why have you disappeared?"

"I just had to tame the beast."

We are all diamonds

In specks of blowing sand.

Like ghosts inside the cosmos

As the time slips through our hands.

We're forgotten, frozen, nothing

We're here, but yet we're damned.

Drifting in the endless ocean

As the time slips through our hands.

"Won't you stay a little longer?"

"I would if this were real."

"Won't you whisper in my ear?"

"I just don't know how I feel."

"Have you become the one in which you should be?"

"I'm fighting for the right."

"Won't you see the shooting star?"

"I'm searching every night."

"How are you my child?"

"I'm trapped inside my mind."

"Are you hurting cos you're lonely?"

"I'm hurting all the time."

"Can you reach out for my hand now?"

"But you're just too far away."

"Will you be coming home soon?"

"I can't I have to stay."

We're all just pathetic creatures

That roam on specks of sand.

Crying always in the nighttime

As the time slips through our hands.

We're flesh and bone and blood

We are here until we're dammed.

Drift aging to the horizon

While the time slips through our hands.

"Do you live in haunted shadow?"

"No, the shadow lives in me."

"Will the endless morning save you?"

"To rip me from my dreams."

"Does the unknown ever grip you?"

"Not when ignorance is bliss."

"Did you try and reach the summit?"

"I'm deep just like a fish."

"Will the moonbeams lacerate your skin?"

"Now I'm drowning in my blood."

"Will the shooting star come back tonight?"

"It's now with you, my love."

"Will you keep crawling, now you've crumbled?"

"Until it breaks my weakening will."

"Won't you stay a little longer?"

"I can't cos it's not real."

The long-forgotten warrior, rides the endless plains

His steed struggles through the sand.

Endless, relentless taunting

As the time slips through our hands.

You want to rip my heart out

But it's not my time to yet be damned.

The rotten souls forgotten

Watching time slip through our hands.

"Are you lost inside this dungeon?"

"I'm lost in my own skin."

"Does the winter leave you frozen?"

"There are icicles within."

"Will you love us for all of time?"

"You are twinkling in my heart."

"Will you swim the raging river?"

"I don't know where it starts."

"Is the shooting star above you?"

"Now it's faded out to dust."

"Is the shooting star still with you?"

"My darling it's with us."

"Can't you stay another moment?"

"I wish that this was real."

"Won't you stay with me forever?"

"If I get the chance, I will."

Rolling silver clouds

That twinkle off the sands.

A soldier fallen in the earth

As the time slips through our hands.

Can we share just one more moment,

Before the day that we are damned?

Let our silent stares be frozen

As time slips right through our hands.

"My precious child are you happy?"

"I know this smile looks pretend."

"My child is this really real?"

"It feels real now and then."

"Do you have a dream to cling to?"

"I've got a nightmare in my head."

"Does endless fear surround you?"

"Fear has nothing left."

"Do you let the wild wind guide you?"

"I let it get me lost."

"Is the Earth so cold beneath you?"

"I'm being eaten by the frost."

"Why did you ever leave us?"

"I had to make my mark."

"Where are you now, this moment?"

"Crouching, huddled in the dark."

We're all like towering giants
That try to control the specks of sand.
Hope is what we cling too
As time slips through our hands.

We're delicate like petals
Of flowers that were damned.
We crumble like the hours
As hours slip right through our hands.

"Can you see the future?"
"All I see is fate."
"Can you be the one we nurture?"
"The one you did create."
"Have you blown your mind again?"
"It's all I ever do."
"Can you leap high like a salmon?"
"If it meant I could reach you."

"Where has the shooting star gone?"

"It's living in my dreams."

"Will you search for it forever?"

"If I can find out what it means."

"Are you flying like an eagle?"

"I'm struggling up the hill."

"Won't you stay a little longer?"

"I can't cos it's not real."

The End

You shine as brightly as a star in the inky cosmos!

If you enjoyed this book, please leave a review on Amazon or Goodreads today!

Check out: Skillfully and beautifully painted across the page, this poetry collection is inspiring, hopeful, and real. Explore your own personal universe in **The Land Behind the Eyes: A Poetry Collection.**

For poetry, and wellbeing posts, connect with me on my website **https://bbrunswickpoetry.com**

Other Works

Out Now!

The Land Behind the Eyes: A Poetry Collection

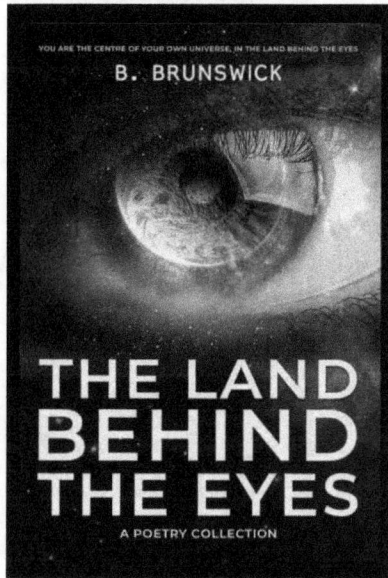

Other Works

Coming Soon!

Here Lies No One: A Poetry Collection